A Joyous Wedding Celebration

VOCAL AND INSTRUMENTAL SELECTIONS

BY

Bryan Jeffery Leech

  Fred Bock Music Company

Foreword

Having contributed wedding songs to two previous collections, *From This Day Forward* (BG0589) and *Whom God Has Joined Together* (BG0670), Fred Bock encouraged me to do an entire wedding book on my own. *I Thank the Lord for Every Single Memory of You* works well as a tribute to parents and is particularly apt just before the entrance of the mothers and groom's father. *Beginning Here Today* and *I Just Saw a Girl* introduce the ceremony to follow. *Grand Entrance* and *Morning Song* provide the needed grandeur for the bride's walk down the aisle. *The Greatest of These Is Love*, based on 1 Corinthians 13, can be used anywhere before or after the vows. *Light a Flame with Me* was written for the candle ceremony. *The Benediction* complements the final prayer and *The Recessional* allows the newly married couple to leave in a moment of majesty and excitement.

One of the thrilling things about being a lyricist/composer is that, vicariously, you are included in countless services by means of the hymns, songs, and anthems you have created. My songs are not songs until you sing them. My marches are only notes on paper until you use them. They'd love to be included in your Day of Days. So please, send them an invitation and include them in your ceremony. They'll make their presence felt and add to the occasion if they're well-performed. So now it's your turn to RSVP.

Have fun preparing. Have a joyous wedding. And have a life together which, at its heart, puts the Lord before everything else.

Bryan Jeffery Leech
Santa Barbara, California
1992

Table of Contents

Fred Bock Music Company

to Randy & Sheryl Thyberg

BEGINNING HERE TODAY

Arranged by Ruth Morris Gray

Words and Music by
Bryan Jeffery Leech

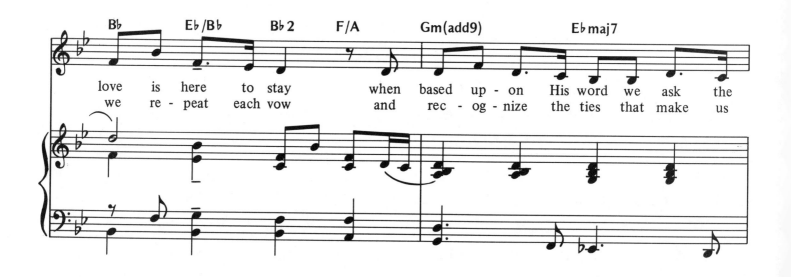

to Robert Plimpton

GRAND ENTRANCE MARCH

Arranged by Edwin T. Childs

Music by Bryan Jeffery Leech

Solo
Trumpet 8'

to Jeff & Robyn Candell

A WEDDING HAS BEGUN

(I JUST SAW A GIRL)

DUET

Arranged by Ruth Morris Gray

Words and Music by
Bryan Jeffery Leech

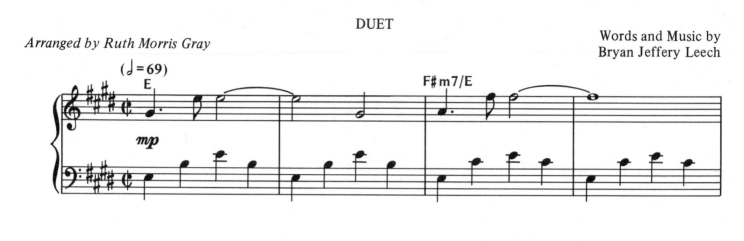

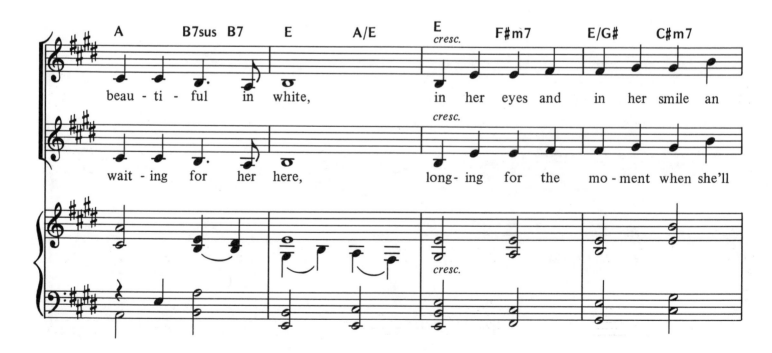

12

Here he'll meet her, here he'll take her hand for - ev - er - more.

Here he'll greet her, here he'll take her hand for - ev - er - more.

As Je - sus long a - go be - came a wed - ding

guest and took the wa - ter giv - en Him and made it in - to

to Douglas Gray, my husband

I'LL LOVE YOU ALL
THE DAYS OF MY LIFE

Words and Music by
Ruth Morris Gray

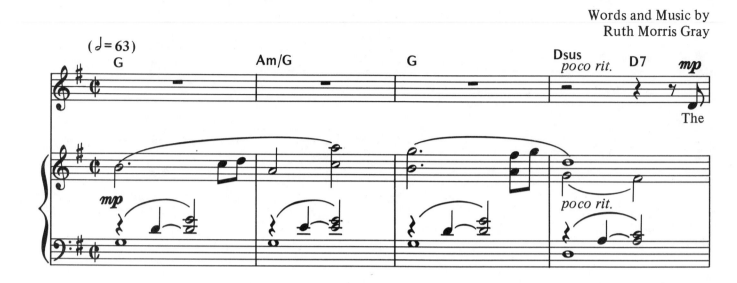

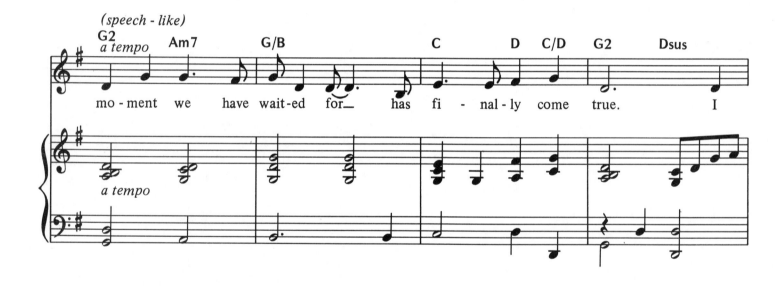

to James & Brenda Colwell

LIGHT A FLAME WITH ME

Words and Music by
Bryan Jeffery Leech

Arranged by Steve Wilkinson

to Gerry & Donna Bouma

THE GIFT OF LOVE
YOU'VE GIVEN US

Arranged by Ruth Morris Gray

Words and Music by
Bryan Jeffery Leech

to David & Cathy Leestma

THE GREATEST OF THESE IS LOVE

Words based on I Corinthians 13
Paraphrased by B.J.L.

Music by
Bryan Jeffery Leech
Arranged by Ruth Morris Gray

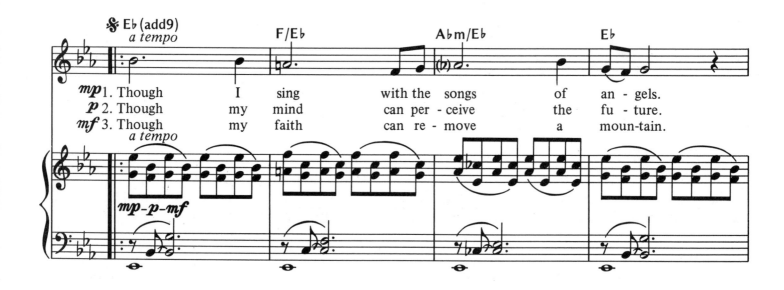

1. Though I sing with the songs of an-gels.
2. Though my mind can per-ceive the fu-ture.
3. Though my faith can re-move a moun-tain.

Though I speak with a sil-ver sound, and have not
Though I know what the mys-t'ries mean, and though I
Though my trust proves the truth of God, and tho' through

I THANK THE LORD FOR EVERY SINGLE MEMORY OF YOU

Arranged by Ruth Morris Gray

Words and Music by
Bryan Jeffery Leech

1. No one has touched my life in quite the way that you have.
2. No one can lift my heart in quite the way that you can.

You've al-ways been be-side me, you've al-ways led the way.
You've had a dream for me, you've nev-er let it die.

You've helped to form my faith, you've wrapped your prayers a-round me.
No one has been more wise or hon-est in their speak-ing.

to Debby Cherry

RECESSIONAL

Music by Bryan Jeffery Leech

Arranged by Edwin T. Childs

Festive (♩ = 124)

to Jeff & Robyn Candell

WEDDING BENEDICTION

Arranged by Ruth Morris Gray

Words and Music by
Bryan Jeffery Leech

to Jane & Martin Guntrip

MORNING SONG
(Processional)

Music by
Bryan Jeffery Leech

PIANO COLLECTIONS
(Medium-Easy to Difficult)
by various arrangers

BOCK'S BEST #1 (BG0557) . . . . Arr. Fred Bock
Fifty arrangements of hymns, gospel songs, and folk-hymns, including Fred Bock's popular setting of *Jesus Loves Me* based on Debussy's *Clair de Lune.*

BOCK'S BEST #2 (BG0572) . . . . Arr. Fred Bock
Fifty hymns and gospel songs --- more of his popular rich-harmonies style of piano writing. This collection includes *My Tribute, A Mighty Fortress is Our God, Easter Song, We Shall Behold Him, The Old Rugged Cross,* and 45 more.

BOCK'S BEST #3 (BG0679) . . . . Arr. Fred Bock
Twenty-five tremendous Christmas piano solos. All your favorites are here: *Silent Night, Go Tell It On the Mountain, O Little Town of Bethlehem, Away in a Manger,* dressed up for the holidays in their best Fred Bock arrangements.

BOCK'S BEST #4 (BG0880) . . . . Arr. Fred Bock
Fifty piano solos featuring Fred Bock's unusual and rich harmonic progressions. You'll enjoy playing these for offertories, preludes, or just for at-the-piano fun. Includes *We Will Glorify, It Is Well with My Soul, Another Time, Another Place, How Majestic is Your Name, The Wedding Song, I Love You, Lord, People Need the Lord, Soon and Very Soon, Give Thanks,* and 41 more excellent titles.

THE GOLDEN COLLECTION (BG0609) . . . . Arr. Rudy Atwood
Concerto-like setting of gospel hymns. Fifty titles, all standards in everyone's hymnal, are presented here in Mr. Atwood's popular and famous style, rich with moving octaves in the left hand. Medium-difficult.

HYMNS IN THE STYLE OF THE MASTERS (BG0744) . . . . Arr. Michelle Murray
Favorite hymns arranged in the style of classical composers. Thematic ideas from composers such as Bach, Beethoven, Chopin, Dvorak and Haydn are woven into hymn settings of *Precious Lord, Take My Hand, How Great thou Art,* and others.

HYMNS IN THE STYLE OF THE MASTERS #2 (BG0868) . . . . . . Arr. Michelle Murray
More hymns, this time in the style of Bach, Schumann, and Liszt. The hymns include *Christ, the Lord is Risen Today, Turn Your Eyes Upon Jesus, We Gather Together,* and Christmas and Patriotic medleys.

PIANO ALIVE! (BG0870) . . . . .Arr. Ted Cornell
Pianist with the Billy Graham Crusades, Mr. Cornell writes in a strong and challenging style. This volume contains *Jesus Shall Reign, Let All Mortal Flesh Keep Silence, All Creatures of Our God and King,* and more.

PRAISE HIM! (BG0766) . . . . .Arr. Ted Cornell
Seven hymn settings including *Beneath the Cross of Jesus, Joyful, Joyful We Adore Thee, Praise Him, Praise Him!, Glorious Things of Thee Are Spoken,* and more.

SACRED PIANO FAVORITES (BG0876) . . . . Arr. Michael Faircloth
Challenging and rewarding piano solos in medium-difficult level. Very usable settings of *Blessed Assurance, In the Garden, It Is Well with My Soul, I Have Decided to Follow Jesus,* and eight more hymns and gospel songs, some in medley format.

Fred Bock Music Company
Available at your local dealer